Contents

Map of Antarctica

Antarctica is the southernmost continent on Earth and the only continent without a native human population. While it has been claimed by a number of countries, those claims have not been officially recognised. Instead, many countries have set up research stations on Antarctica. These countries are signatories to the Antarctic Treaty.

Australia's Neighbours

Antarctica

DISCOVER THE LAND, HISTORY AND PEOPLE

Jane Hinchey

REDBACK publishing

First published 2019 by
Redback Publishing
PO Box 357 Frenchs Forest NSW 2086
Australia

www.redbackpublishing.com.au
orders@redbackpublishing.com.au

978-1-925860-69-6

Author: Jane Hinchey
Editor: Marianne Lindsell
Designer: Redback Publishing

Original illustrations © Redback Publishing 2019
Originated by Redback Publishing

Printed and bound in China by Leo Paper

MIX
Paper from responsible sources
FSC® C020056
FSC
www.fsc.org

Acknowledgements
Abbreviations: l—left, r—right, b—bottom, t—top, c—centre, m—middle
We would like to thank the following for permission to reproduce photographs: (Images © shutterstock) p12m EhayDy, p17 polarman, p26b chrisontour84

NATIONAL LIBRARY OF AUSTRALIA
A catalogue record for this book is available from the National Library of Australia

The Australian Antarctic Territory (AAT) was claimed by the United Kingdom and placed under the authority of the Commonwealth of Australia in 1933. It covers 42% of the continent and is by far the largest claim in the region of any nation.

Snapshot

Official name:	Australian Antarctic Territory (AAT)
Government:	Australian external territory
Total area:	5.9 million square kilometres
Capital:	Davis Station
Currency:	Australian dollar
Population:	Less than 1,000
Largest research station:	Mirny Station (Russia)
Sovereign state:	Australia
Chief Scientist:	Gwen Fenton
Highest point:	Mawson Peak at 2,745 metres

Fun Facts

- Antarctica is the largest desert in the world.
- The coldest place on Earth is one area of Antarctica, where temperatures can drop below -93 degrees celcius.
- There are no fully terrestrial amphibians, mammals or reptiles on Antarctica.
- Antarctica was once covered in forest and inhabited by many species of animals including dinosaurs.
- 90% of the world's fresh water is in Antarctica.

FAST FACT!

Ships take between 10 to12 days to reach Davis Station from Hobart.

Meet the Neighbour: Antarctica

Antarctica is the coldest, driest, and windiest continent on Earth. 98% of the continent is covered with ice and no tundra, trees or bushes grow here. Only about 1% of the continent is permanently ice-free. This is the subantarctic region, immediately north of the Antarctic region.

Antarctica is Earth's only continent without a native human population. The majority of Antarctica is claimed by one or more countries, although these claims are not officially recognised. In 1961, 12 countries agreed to enforce the Antarctic Treaty. They were Argentina, Australia, Belgium, Chile, France, Japan, New Zealand, Norway, South Africa, the Soviet Union, the United Kingdom and the USA.

Between them, these countries had already established over 50 Antarctic stations, so the treaty was a formalisation of the existing cooperation that had been established between these countries' operational and scientific communities. The treaty now has 53 parties.

Australian Antarctic Territory

Australian Antarctic Territory (AAT) is a part of Antarctica that is administered by Australia. Overseeing it is the Australian Antarctic Division, which is an agency of the federal government's Department of Environment and Energy.

The Australian Antarctic Territory covers nearly 5.9 million square kilometres, about 42% of Antarctica and the subantarctic islands of Macquarie, Heard and McDonald. The population is less than 1,000.

The Australian Antarctic Division maintains four permanent research stations that are occupied year round by scientists and support staff.

- Mawson, Davis and Casey are on the Antarctic continent.
- Macquarie Island is in the subantarctic.

The Division also manages Heard and McDonald Islands, Commonwealth Bay and keeps a weather station at Dome A, the highest point in Antarctica.

The Territory of Heard Island and McDonald Islands

Heard and McDonald Islands are Australian external territories located in the Southern Ocean, closer to Antarctica than to Australia. The islands have been Australian territories since 1947. Although unknown to most Australians, the Islands are Australia's only sovereign territories in the Southern Indian Ocean sector of the globe.

The islands are barren and volcanic. There are no ports or harbours and the islands are surrounded by dangerous waters, so are difficult to reach and inhospitable for humans. Because there has been very little human interference on the islands, they remain in pristine condition, with undamaged ecosystems and no introduced plant or animal species. The flora and fauna of Heard and McDonald Islands have evolved naturally. Because of this, these unique islands received a World Heritage Listing in 1997.

Did You Know?

Australia's only two active volcanoes are found in The Territory of Heard and McDonald Islands.

Government and International Treaties

Antarctica does not have its own government, nor does it belong to one country, although there are numerous pending historical claims. Governance is carried out by 29 consultative nations at an annual Antarctic Treaty Consultative Meeting.

Each of the consultative nations has one or more bases on the continent. Each Antarctic base is governed by the national laws of its home country.

Antarctic Treaty

July 1957 to December 1958 was known as the International Geophysical Year. At this time there were 12 countries active in Antarctica. These countries were Argentina, Australia, Belgium, Chile, France, Japan, New Zealand, Norway, South Africa, the USSR, the United Kingdom and the United States of America. These countries were invited by the USA to a conference where a treaty to ensure, in the interests of all mankind, that Antarctica shall continue forever to be used exclusively for peaceful purposes and shall not become the scene or object of international discord.

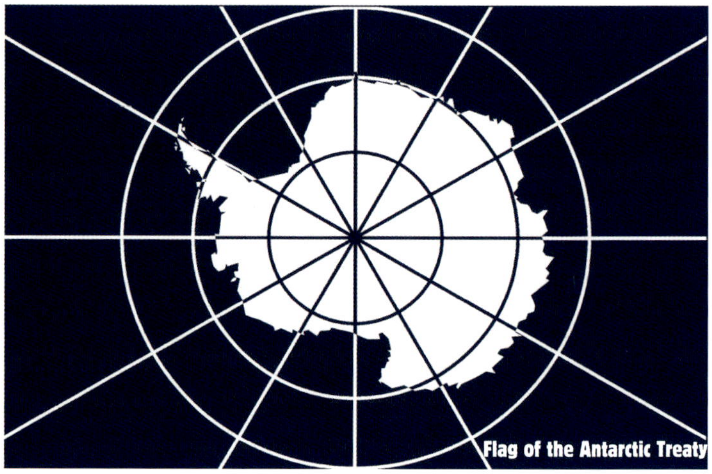
Flag of the Antarctic Treaty

These original 12 nations were later joined by Brazil, Bulgaria, the People's Republic of China, Ecuador, Finland, Germany, India, Italy, South Korea, Netherlands, Peru, Poland, Spain, Sweden and Uruguay to form the Consultative Parties. There are also 24 Non-Consultative Parties who are signatories to the treaty.

The treaty is a short document focussing on peace, cooperation, non-nuclearisation, free exchange of scientific results, and territorial sovereignty, preventing new claims and setting aside arguments over the existing ones. The Antarctic Treaty came into effect in 1961, dedicating the continent to peaceful scientific investigation. All territorial claims were suspended. A total of 53 countries have now signed the treaty, which has resulted in Antarctica being a peaceful place, that has never affected by war.

Consultative Nations

United Kingdom, South Africa, Belgium, Japan, United States of America, Norway, France, New Zealand, Russia, Poland, Argentina, Australia, Chile, Netherlands, Germany, Brazil, Bulgaria, Uruguay, Italy, Peru, Spain, China, India, Sweden, Finland, Korea, Ecuador, Ukraine.

Madrid Protocol

In 1991, the parties of the Antarctic Treaty came together to sign the Madrid Protocol, which is the framework for protecting the Antarctic environment. This designates Antarctica as a natural reserve, devoted to peace and science and requires that care for the environment is a fundamental consideration in all activities.

The Committee for Environmental Protection (CEP) was established under the Madrid Protocol, comprising of members from all the countries that are party to the protocol. The CEP currently:

- prevents the introduction of non-native species to Antarctica
- manages the environmental implications of climate change
- addresses how Antarctic tourism interacts with the environment
- addresses environmental challenges from activities conducted before the Madrid Protocol entered into force. These include the clean-up of past waste disposal sites and abandoned facilities
- the development of Antarctic protected areas.

Historical Claims

Seven countries have laid claim to parts of Antarctica, but any conflict for sovereignty, and any new claims cannot occur while The Antarctic Treaty is in force.

Among the original signatories of the Antarctic Treaty were the seven countries with territorial claims. Most Treaty Parties do not recognise the territorial claims made by these seven countries, and others maintain they reserve the right to make a claim.

The seven historical claims to parts of Antarctica, some overlapping, are:

- Argentina
- Australia
- Chile
- France
- New Zealand
- Norway
- United Kingdom.

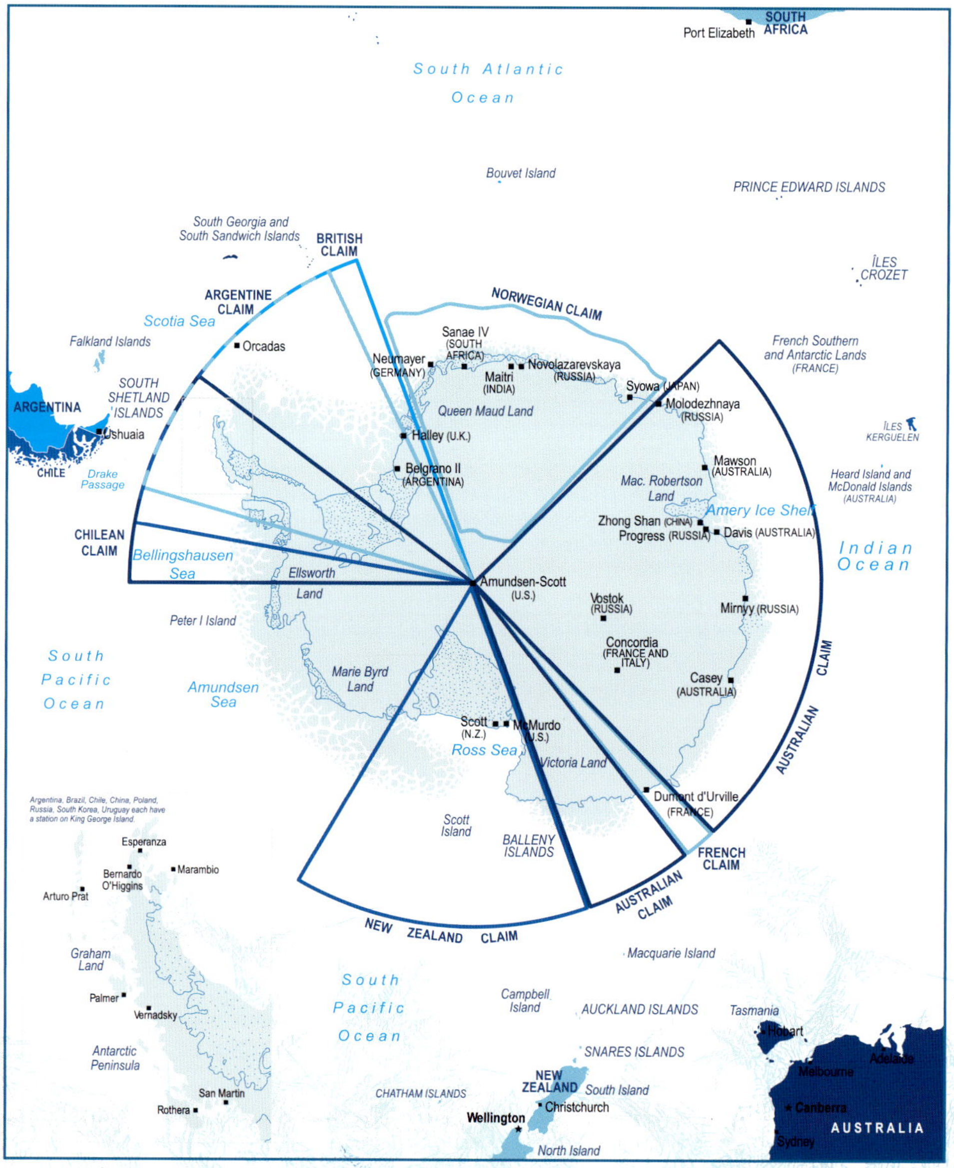

Fast Fact!

Only four countries recognise Australia's claim to sovereignty in Antarctica:

- New Zealand
- France
- Norway
- United Kingdom.

The Territory of Heard Island and McDonald Islands

No one lives on these islands. Since the first landing on Heard Island in 1855, human activity in the area has been limited. There have been approximately 240 landings on Heard Island and only two landings on McDonald Island, in 1971 and 1980. Early landings on Heard Island were due to sealing in the area, but more recently visits have been for research and scientific purposes.

Shore parties consist of scientists and some support crew who set up camps for anything from a few weeks to a few months. The Australian Antarctic Division has also performed environmental management activities, such as removing waste material from Atlas Cove. Most waste is returned to Australia to be dealt with.

There have been only a few private landings on Heard Island. Numbers remain small despite the growth in numbers to other subantarctic and Antarctic sites.

Research in the area focuses on climate change and the impact on the biodiversity and ecosystems of Heard Island. Research disciplines include:

- geology
- vulcanology
- ecology
- glaciology
- geomorphology
- meteorology
- terrestrial and marine ecology
- oceanography
- cultural and heritage study.

Timeline

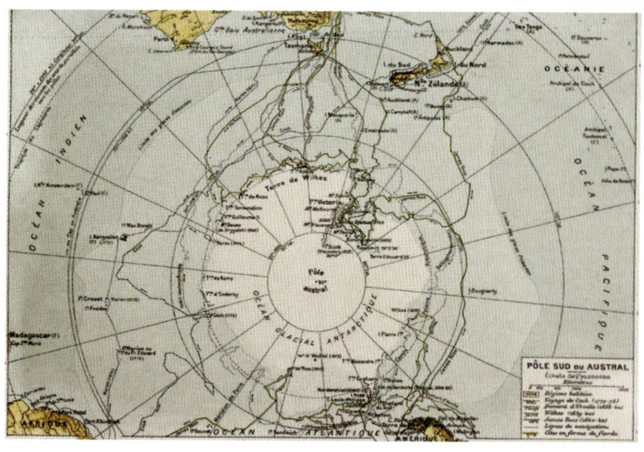

1772 to 1775

James Cook becomes the first person to navigate across the Antarctic Circle.

1819 to 1820

James Bransfield sighted the Antarctic Peninsula.

1800s

Much of the early exploration was about finding good hunting grounds for seals. In the 1890s Norwegian and Scottish expeditions explored the area for whaling.

Early 1900s

Many countries sent exploring expeditions to the Antarctic. The Norwegian explorer Roald Amundsen was the first to reach the South Pole on 14 December 1911.

1907 to 1909

Ernest H. Shackleton and his team, which included legendary Australian explorer, Douglas Mawson, carried out extensive research work.

1911 to 1914

The Australasian Antarctic Expedition (AAE) with Mawson, set up huts and bases, and established the first radio communications in Antarctica. They successfully charted large segments of the east Antarctic coastline, and investigated sub-antarctic Macquarie Island and the Southern Ocean.

1929 to 1931

Mawson followed this up with the British, Australian and New Zealand Antarctic Research Expedition (BANZARE).

Mid 1900s

Explorers from many countries visited Antarctica during the early half of the century. In 1957, Antarctic exploration and scientific studies became the focus of the International Geophysical Year (IGY).

1954

Australia established Mawson, its first permanent station on the Antarctic continent.

1961

IGY led to the establishment of the Antarctic Treaty, which has been signed by 53 countries. It also promotes peace and international scientific cooperation on the continent.

1998

The Madrid Protocol enters into force, designating Antarctica's 'natural reserve devoted to peace and science' and prohibiting mining in Antarctica.

Mawson Station

People and Daily Life

Antarctica does not have cities or any towns as we know them. It does not have an indigenous or permanent population. Anyone who lives there does so because they work on scientific research stations or bases.

Spread across the continent are about 70 research stations. The 29 countries that signed the Antarctic Treaty are allowed to maintain a seasonal or year-round station in the Antarctic. Some countries maintain both statuses. There are about 4,000 people working in Antarctica through the summer months and about 1,000 over winter each year.

Working in Antarctica is not like most jobs. People don't commute there, or even fly in and out on short contracts. Contracts range from six months over the summer months, to up to 15 months.

Despite the isolation, many people see working in Antarctica as a dream job; a once in a lifetime opportunity. In 2017, about 2,500 people applied for 160 positions at the Australian Antarctic Division.

Australia Antarctic Territory

Australia has four permanent Antarctic research stations — Casey, Davis and Mawson on the continent, as well as Macquarie Island in the subantarctic. They are occupied year-round, although staff levels drop significantly over the winter.

There are about 470 people working on Australia's Antarctic Program. One in five are scientists, but there are also others who work in trades and support roles.

Some of the jobs available are:

- Electricians
- Plumbers
- Carpenters
- Chefs
- Doctors.

Australian Antarctic Division Base Macquarie Island

Fun Fact!

At least ten children have been born in West Antarctica.

The Stations

Australia has four stations: Casey, Mawson, Davis and Macquarie Island. These stations are home to many people living in otherwise harsh and isolated conditions. So the living quarters and facilities are comfortable. Each expeditioner usually has his or her own room called a donga, although over the busier summer period, some people have to share. There are communal sitting areas and a dining hall, as well as laundry facilities.

While each station differs, some of the facilities at the stations might include:

- a ski loop nearby
- some outdoor sporting areas
- a cinema
- a hydroponic garden
- a medical centre
- table tennis and pool tables
- a library
- a store
- a gym and cardio room
- a brewery and a bar
- a spa
- a sauna
- a climbing wall
- musical instruments and facilities for a band and performances
- hobby huts to use for arts and crafts.

Fast Fact!

The most populous Antarctic centre is McMurdo Base on Ross Island, operated by the United States of America.

Children on Antarctica

Esperanza is an Argentinian base built in 1951, that expanded in 1978. Silvia Morello de Palma, the wife of Esperanza's station leader, was flown in when she was seven months pregnant. The idea was to claim sovereignty by giving birth to the first native-born Antarctican. On January 7, 1978 she gave birth to Emilio Marcos de Palma. Over the next five years, four more boys and three girls were born here. Today, around 20 children live with their families at Esperanza, with its family atmosphere and facilities making it more like a village than scientific station.

Countries With Antarctic Research Stations:

Argentina	Ecuador	Norway	Spain
Australia	Finland	Pakistan	Sweden
Belgium	France	Peru	Ukraine
Brazil	Germany	Poland	United Kingdom
Bulgaria	India	Romania	United States of America
Chile	Italy	Russia	Uruguay
China	Japan	South Africa	
Czech Republic	New Zealand	South Korea	

Clothing

Buildings at the research stations are heated to 18 degrees Celsius all year round, so the residents can wear normal clothes such as jeans and t-shirts. Outdoor clothing depends on what season it is, but generally includes insulating layers such as long woollen underwear, trousers and a shirt, and outer layers that are windproof and waterproof. Gloves and headgear are essential outside. It's important to not get so hot that you sweat, because the moisture created can cause your clothes to freeze. All clothes required for work are provided by the AAD. There is a clothing store at each station.

Food

Food is prepared by qualified chefs in commercial style kitchens. Food is stored carefully to maintain freshness between supply ships. Station meals are similar to what people eat at home in Australia. While there might not be as much fresh produce available, and any fresh food that comes from Australia has spent weeks on a ship, each station houses hydroponics facilities that ensure a steady supply of herbs, fruits and vegetables. Snacks, sweets and nuts are also supplied.

Whopper Shopper!

The 2016-17 shopping list for all stations included:

Bacon	1,310 kg
Beef eye fillet	457 kg
Chicken	2,961 kg
Frozen peas	864 kg
Ice cream	1,980 litres
Coffee beans	546 kg
Potatoes	4,800 kg
Fresh eggs (oiled)	34,560
Chocolate	864 kg
Cheese	2,262 kg
Toilet paper	1,920 rolls
Total frozen and +4°C food (no dry goods)	51,976 kg

Antarctic Veggie Gardens

Crops grown at Australian stations include: Cucumbers, zucchinis, spinach, tomatoes, lettuces, capsicums, beans, snow peas, fennel, coriander and basil.

Getting Involved

While everyone on an Antarctic station has a job, they are also expected to participate in station duties. These duties include housekeeping and general maintenance and are allocated on a rotating roster.

As well as general duties there are many volunteer roles available, to encourage residents to be more involved in the station community.

Volunteer station positions may include roles such as:

- firefighters and theatre nurses
- officers in charge of flags, work, health and safety, and the gym
- coordinators for station news, hydroponics, search and rescue, and IT
- librarian, postal agent, and hairdresser.

Sports

Antarctica and sports don't immediately seem compatible; however the residents of this harsh continent are generally sports conscious. All the stations contain gyms, and often climbing walls and cardio rooms. A diverse range of classes such as yoga, basketball and fencing keep the expeditionists fit in winter. Then, during the milder summer months, an array of outdoor sporting activities begin, from skiing, hiking, and team sports such as rugby, softball and cricket.

Since 2006, Antarctica has played host to dozens of cold-weather loving runners from across the globe. The Antarctic Ice Marathon and 100 kilometre Ultra-marathon are gruelling events held across a large stretch of ice near the South Pole.

Transport

There are a number of different modes of transport at the stations, including cranes, loaders and machinery to help lift supplies from boats. Field support vehicles include snow mobiles, sleds and all terrain carriers. Expeditioners using any of the station vehicles must first undergo basic training in how to drive in the frozen conditions, along with learning essential emergency procedures.

Geography and Climate

Antarctica is made up of one major landmass, twice the size of Australia, and a number of smaller islands. It is surrounded by the Southern Ocean. About 98% of the continent is covered by an ice sheet that in some areas is over 4 kilometres deep. Under the ice are mountains, valleys and plains. In 2017, massive landforms were found under the ice, including three canyons, larger than the Grand Canyon. There are more than 400 known lakes, including Lake Vostok, the world's sixth largest lake. Mount Erebus, standing at 3,794 meters high, and there is an active volcano located in East Antarctica, on the edge of the Ross Ice Shelf.

The Southern Ocean

The Southern Ocean surrounds the mainland of Antarctica. It is home to whales, seals and fish. Birds such as penguins and albatross all live in or rely on these waters. Antarctic ice fish have an antifreeze protein that keeps their blood flowing.

The Southern Ocean will often have ice floating in it. Close to the mainland are huge floating pieces of sea ice, called pack ice. It forms during the winter, more than doubling the size of the Antarctic continent, and then melts in the spring and summer. It is not attached to a shoreline and can be moved by the wind and ocean currents. Climate change impacts pack ice and the animals that live and feed around it.

Icebergs are enormous bodies of ice that break off glaciers or ice shelves. Even the small ones weigh hundreds of tonnes, so they can be dangerous to ships.

CLIMATE

Antarctica is the coldest, windiest, and driest continent on Earth. The average winter temperature from March to September is -60°Celcius, while the average summer temperature from October to February is -31°Celcius. The record low temperature in Antarctica is -89.6°Celcius.

Ice Free

When you think of Antarctica, you probably picture ice and glaciers, and you would be mainly right. Yet most Antarctic animals live in the permanently ice-free areas that cover about 1% of the continent. This is the subantarctic region, immediately north of the Antarctic region.

Islands

There are many small islands in the Australian Antarctic Territory, and elsewhere in the region. Some are ice free, while others are covered in glaciers.

McDonald Island

Located 44 kilometres to the west of Heard Island, the McDonald Islands are small, totalling about 2.5 square kilometres. The main island has a sloping plateau on the northern side while the south side is a steep hill. The smaller islands are rocky islets.

The volcano on McDonald Island was dormant for 75,000 years and became active again in 1992. It has erupted several times since then.

A survey of the island in 1980 showed that the McDonald Island's plant life was less diverse than that of Heard Island. Four mosses and a number of algae species were recorded, along with some fungi.

On McDonald Island, 23 species of marine mammals can be found, including seals, whales, dolphins and a porpoise. There are 11 species of birds that are similar to the birds on Heard Island.

Heard Island

The largest of the group of islands, Heard Island is mountainous, dominated by Big Ben, an active volcano that at 2,475 metres high dwarfs any mountain on mainland Australia.

The island is 80% covered by ice, including 41 glaciers. Microfossil records show that ferns and woody plants were once present on the island around 65 million to 2.58 million years ago. However, they don't exist there today. Heard Island has the smallest number of plant species of any of the subantarctic islands groups, which reveals just how isolated it is. Flora includes low-growing herbaceous flowering plants and vegetation, and numerous moss and algae species.

Fast Fact!

15 species of flying birds, including the endangered Southern Giant Petrel, use Heard Island as a breeding ground.

Fast Fact!

Australia's only two active volcanoes are found in The Territory of Heard and McDonald Islands.

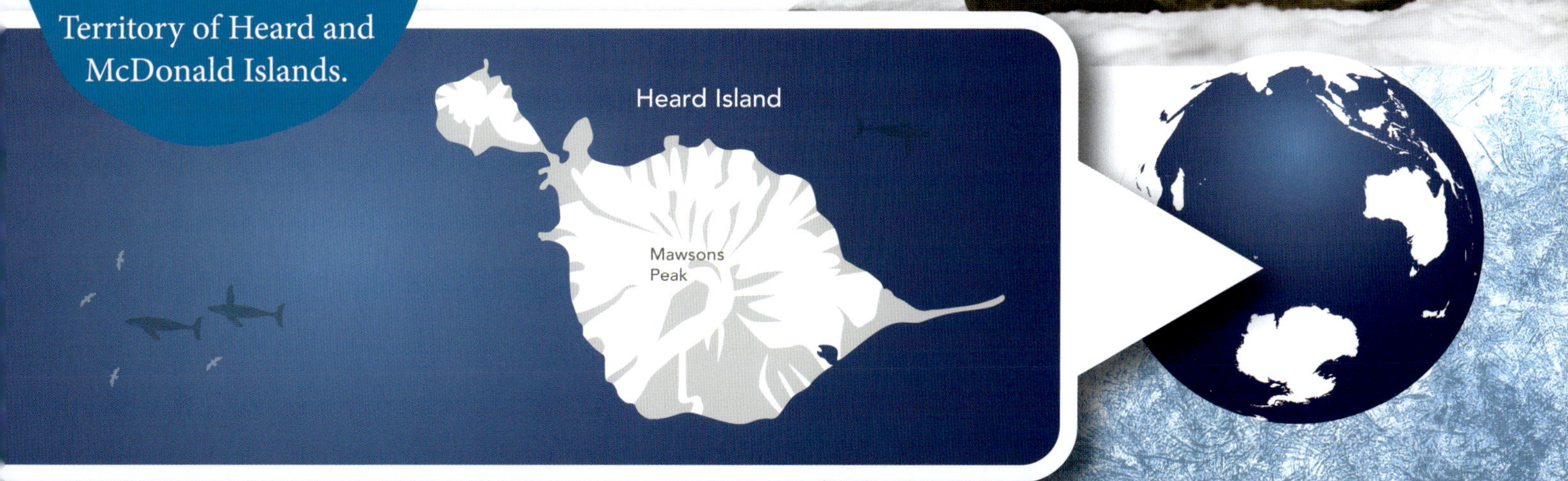

Wildlife

Antarctica is home to a wide range of penguins, whales, seals, krill, land invertebrates and seabirds such as albatross and terns.

In 1991, the parties of the Antarctic Treaty came together to sign the Madrid Protocol, which is the framework for protecting the Antarctic environment. This designates Antarctica as a natural reserve, devoted to peace and science and requires that care for the environment is a fundamental consideration in all activities.

Fast Fact!

Around 88% of species in the Southern Ocean are found nowhere else in the world.

Adapting to the Cold

Antarctic animals survive the freezing conditions by reducing the amount of body heat that they may lose. This can be through behaviours, such as huddling together like the emperor penguins, or by physical means that has evolved over time. Some of these physical adaptations include:

- a thick waterproof and windproof coats: Many Antarctic animals such as emperor penguins have coats that protect them from freezing water and wind.
- a thick layer of fat: Whales, seals and some penguins have layers of blubber that insulate them from the freezing conditions. Male elephant seals can use their blubber as an energy reserve and live off their fat reserves during summer.
- extremities such as bills and flippers that are smaller, meaning less blood is needed for these areas, and therefore less heat is lost.

Whales

Threats to whale populations include climate change, underwater noise pollution, fishing nets, widespread plastic pollution and ship strikes. Whales have a very slow reproductive rate with adult females giving birth to one calf every few years. Australian waters are an important habitat for many species of whales. Five whale species are currently listed under Australia's Environment Protection and Biodiversity Conservation Act (EPBC) as nationally threatened, and all are found in the Southern Ocean.

- blue whale (Endangered)
- southern right whale (Vulnerable)
- sei whale (Endangered)
- fin whale (Endangered)
- humpback whale (Least Concern)

Blue Whale

The blue whale is the largest of all whales and the largest animal to ever live on Earth. Blue whales are blue to blue-grey and grow up to about 30 metres in length and weigh about 200 tonnes. They migrate between their Antarctic summer feeding grounds and their winter breeding grounds. They travel long distances to find the huge amounts of krill, their sole source of food, needed to survive. The blue whale is listed as Endangered.

Penguins

There are 18 species of penguins and all are restricted to the Southern Hemisphere, with most on the Antarctic coasts and subantarctic islands.
Penguins feed on small fish and krill, catching these one at a time. They are also food themselves, for animals such as killer whales and leopard seals. On land, carnivorous birds steal their eggs and chicks.

The Royal Penguin

The royal penguin has a distinct crest of yellow and black feathers. From their face down they have white feathers, while their back is black. They only breed on Macquarie Island. While they are currently thriving on the island, they are listed as Near Threatened because of their extremely limited breeding area. Any damage to Macquarie Island and the penguin's habitat, and the royal penguin numbers could decrease quickly.

Albatross

Antarctica and the subantarctic islands are home to a wide range of seabirds, including petrels, terns, gulls, albatrosses, shearwaters, cormorants, gannets and boobies.

There are 22 species of albatross, and 21 of these species occur in the Southern Hemisphere. 19 of these species occur in Australian waters, and five breed in Australia.

Four areas within Australian waters have been listed as critical habitat for the albatrosses. Macquarie Island is listed as critical habitat for the wandering and grey-headed albatrosses.

Albatrosses have one of the lowest reproductive rates of any bird. All species of albatross lay a single egg. This, and the threats to their environment puts the albatrosses at risk.

The Importance of Krill

The Antarctic ecosystem relies on krill. This tiny shrimp-like organism is the key prey species for many creatures, including fish, seal, seabirds and whales. Blue whales can eat four tonnes of krill a day while baleen whales can consume thousands of tonnes. Countless species are dependent on krill, which means that if the krill population was compromised, all other species would be impacted.

The Wandering Albatross

The wandering albatross is the largest of seabirds, with a wing-span reaching three metres. It can stay at sea for up to a month in search of fish and squid, often covering in excess of 10,000 kilometres on its journey.

Endangered, Threatened and Vulnerable

Many species of animals that live and breed in Antarctica are now under threat, due to global warming, increased fishing and tourism, marine pollution and invasive species.

Wildlife Warrior Activity

Choose one Endangered animal species that lives in Antarctica and research what is being done to protect it. Can you think of any other ways to protect this animal?

Animals under threat:

Critically Endangered

Amsterdam Albatross
Tristan Albatross

Endangered

Sei Whale
Blue Whale
Fin Whale
Northern Royal Albatross
Sooty Albatross
Indian Yellow-nosed Albatross
Grey-headed Albatross
Abbott's Booby

Near Threatened

Magellanic Penguin
Emperor Penguin
Adelie Penguin
Gentoo Penguin
Buller's Albatross
Shy Albatross
White-capped Albatross

Vulnerable

Rockhopper Penguin
Macaroni Penguin
Antipodean Albatross
Southern Royal Albatross
Wandering Albatross
Chatham Albatross
Campbell Albatross
Salvin's Albatross
Southern Right Whale

Least Concern

Humpback Whale
King Penguin

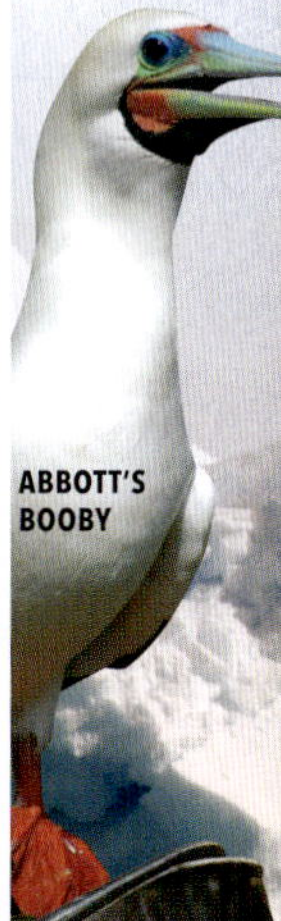

Tourism

Visitors are flocking to Antarctica. To reduce the impact of this growing trend, annual numbers are capped. In 2016-2017, there were 44,202 visitors.

A trip to Antarctica is expensive, so is a once-in-a-lifetime adventure for many who visit. However, the spectacular, pristine landscapes and an abundance of incredible wildlife, that are often unafraid of humans, make this a very worthwhile journey.

By Ship

Most cruises leave from Ushuaia, located on the southernmost tip of Argentina, and South America. The shorter cruises take about 12 days, travelling through the Drake Passage to the Antarctic Peninsula and back. Some cruises are longer and incorporate activities such as mountaineering and camping. Most cruise passengers have the opportunity to experience wildlife up-close with shore excursions and activities such as kayaking.

While departures from South America are more common, it is possible to cruise from Invercargill in New Zealand and Hobart in Tasmania, Australia. These cruises take about 21 days and include visits to remote islands such as Macquarie, Snares, Auckland and Campbell.

The Antarctica season runs from late October until late March.

By Plane

Some people decide to fly over the Drake Passage rather than sail through it. Flights to King George Island are more common now, with travellers joining boats once they're there. These are called fly-cruise options.

Map It Activity

Using a map of Australia, Antarctica and New Zealand, can you chart the cruise itinerary below?

- Hobart
- Macquarie Island
- Cape Denison
- Campbell Island
- Auckland Islands
- The Snares
- Invercargill

Threats to Antarctica

There are a number of major issues impacting Antarctica.

Climate Change

Climate change is the greatest threat to Antarctica. Temperatures on Antarctica's west coast have risen by 3 degrees celsius since the mid-20th Century. Global warming and a rise in sea temperatures will impact land and sea ice. Already, some huge shelves of ice have collapsed and glaciers have diminished in size. This will affect Antarctic and subantarctic habitats in numerous ways including directly altered weather patterns and rising sea levels. These events could disrupt the normal cycle of variability to which animals and plants have adapted. Increased emissions of CO_2 to the atmosphere are partly absorbed by oceans, which increases the acidity of ocean waters and changes the physiology of marine organisms. Rising sea temperatures will also affect microscopic plankton, resulting in changes to the whole ocean ecosystem.

Research shows that ice-free areas in Antarctica could expand by close to 25% by 2100. This would drastically change the animal and plant life of the continent.

Changing Ecosystems

An animal's survival often depends on the animal's ecosystem maintaining balance. Any change to the ecosystem can impact the species living there. One example of this is the food chain. The loss of the smallest creature can impact the larger creatures that feed off them, all the way to the top of the food chain. These interconnected food webs are an essential part of the overall ecosystem. Even the smallest change in an ecosystem can have a major impact.

Human Interference

People have been visiting Antarctica for over 100 years. Although there are now treaties in place that provide strict guidelines on what activities can take place there, and how to treat the environment, this wasn't always the case. Hunting for seals and whales, and fishing began in the 18th century. Early exploration teams left their mark on the formerly pristine environment. After the signing of the Antarctic Treaty, countries were responsible for cleaning up human waste; however each country did this in different ways. Some removed the waste from the continent, others simply buried it.

Under the Madrid Protocol, waste produced at research camps must now be disposed of in ice pits or shipped back to Australia. In recent years, waste from the past has also been removed.

Tourism – The Last Frontier

Tourism to Antarctica is rising rapidly. To reduce the impact of this growing trend, annual numbers are capped. In 2016-2017, there were 44,202 visitors. A visit could unknowingly bring in foreign seeds or spores that introduce an alien species to this pristine environment. Therefore all care is taken.

Overfishing

Large scale fishing began in the 1970s. Many species were hunted or fished to near extinction. Birds like albatross and petrels were caught in fishing lines and nets. Fishing for krill, a fish essential to the overall food web, peaked at 500,000 tonnes in the early 1980s.

While the Southern Ocean experiences less fishing than other oceans, due to expense and dangerous sea conditions, it is still overfished. In 1980 the Commission on the Conservation of the Antarctic Marine Living Resources began and the members started meeting annually to discuss the conservation of marine species in the area. The Convention does not prohibit fishing, but it does focus on managing the fisheries. Nowadays, fishing boats must have a license, which sets a specific area and time period to fish, and the species and catch that is allowed. Boats must contain satellite-monitoring devices that can communicate their location. Failure to do so can result in the revoking of the license.

Plastics in Antarctica

Most litter takes hundreds of years to break down, during which time it continues to pollute the ocean and damage marine life. Items such as plastic bags and rings from plastic 'six-packs' can entangle or get eaten by animals, including fish, marine birds, dolphins, whales, and seals.

Up to 12.7 million tonnes of plastic waste is washed into the world's oceans each year. There are now more than 46,000 pieces of plastic floating in every 2.5 square kilometres of the ocean. These plastics are wreaking havoc with marine animals. Ocean currents can shift dangerous pollution hundreds of kilometres from its original source. Plastic debris kills more than one million seabirds every year, as well as more than 100,000 marine mammals.

For a long time scientists thought that Antarctic waters remained plastic free, however recent research shows that the Southern Ocean is also contaminated by plastics. In fact, the problem there is far worse than ever imagined.

Other plastic products such as soda bottles or plastic bags can also break down into miniscule particles creating pieces of microplastic. This impacts the wildlife in the area, specifically the krill which are the foundation of the food chain. The krill then pass harmful chemicals on to all the animals that consume them.

Scientists have estimated that approximately 500 kilograms of microplastics from personal care products and nearly 30 billion clothing fibres make their way into the Southern Ocean each decade. This will rise, with more research activities, fishing and tourism in the region.

What are Microplastics?

A major environmental concern is the use of microplastics, or microbeads. Many modern cosmetics and household products contain tiny particles of plastic that have a devastating impact on marine life.

These products include:

- facial scrub
- body scrub
- toothpaste
- deodorant
- lipstick
- eyeliner
- washing detergent
- cleaning products.

What Can You Do?

Antarctica might seem too far away to help, but actually your day-to-day actions can make a huge difference.

Everyday Changes

- Use less energy and use green energy where possible. The more sustainable your life is, the less you are contributing to climate change.
- When you fly, offset your travel with carbon credits.
- Use public transport and cut back on petrol.
- Eat less meat and buy locally produced produce when you can.
- Cut back on chemical use. Household, garden and agricultural chemicals end up in our river systems and ultimately the ocean.
- Never litter. Pick up any rubbish you see on the beach.
- Cut back on plastic use, including plastic bags, straws and balloons.
- Recycle. The less that is made and consumed, the less CO_2 emissions impact the environment.

Demand Action

- Support meaningful climate action by supporting politicians, organisations and companies that actively address climate change.
- Educate yourself about the Antarctic Treaty, Madrid Protocol and help ensure these, or similar treaties remain in place.
- Choose wisely which goods and services you consume and be vocal about corporations that are placing the planet at risk.

Flags, Symbols, Emblems and Special Days

Flag of New Antarctica

The official flag of Antarctica was adopted in 2002. It has a white map of the continent at the centre of a blue background. The flag is in the ratio of 2:3 and is the official symbol of the continent. The colours represent the continent and its surrounding oceans and also symbolise Antarctica's international neutrality.

Graham Bartram designed the official flag of Antarctica.

Territorial Flags

Countries with research bases on the continent also fly their own national flags, or modified versions of their national flags. The Australian national flag is used in the Australian Antarctic Territory.

Special Days

Each research station celebrates numerous national public holidays throughout the year. Stations in the Australian Antarctic Territory acknowledge a number of special days including Australia Day on 26 January.

Find Out More

Primary and Secondary Sources

A primary source is information created by someone who was a part of or witnessed the historical event first hand. Primary sources are very important to historians researching events and time periods. Examples of primary sources are letters, emails, filmed interviews and clips, journals and diaries, census statistics, government documents, art and maps (from the time period), the news (both print and film), photographs and modern maps.

A secondary source is when someone who did not actually witness the event retells the facts that someone else told them. Examples of secondary sources include news (both print and film), interviews, letters, journals and diaries, biographies, textbooks, paraphrased quotations.

Sources

Australia Antarctic Division - http://www.antarctica.gov.au
Cool Antarctica - http://www.coolantarctica.com

Search Key Words

extinct, endangered, threatened species, vulnerable species, habitats, conservation, ecosystem, sustainability, biodiversity, Antarctic, subantarctic, Heard Island, McDonald Islands, Macquarie Island

History Search

Find examples of primary and secondary sources about the signing of the Madrid Protocol.

Read

Surviving Antarctica, by Andrea White
Endangered Animals and their Habitats: Antarctica by Jane Hinchey

Glossary

ANTARCTIC TREATY: an international treaty that made Antarctica a place for peaceful, scientific research

BLUE WHALE: the largest creature on earth

COOK, CAPTAIN JAMES: the first person to cross the Antarctic Circle

CRITICAL: at a turning point for survival

ECOSYSTEM: the living and non-living parts of an area and the interactions between them

ENDANGERED: may soon become extinct

ENDEMIC: only found in a certain place

EXTINCT: no longer in existence

FERAL PREDATORS: non-native animals that kill and eat other animals

GLACIER: a river of ice

HABITAT: place where plants and animals live

ICEBERGS: huge pieces of floating ice

ICE CLIFF: walls of ice where glaciers meet the sea

PACK ICE: floating pieces of sea ice

RECOVERY PLAN: a plan for the conservation of a species

SPECIES: one kind of living thing

TERRITORIAL CLAIMS: when a country says it owns part of Antarctica

THREAT: anything that may reduce the numbers of a species

THREATENED: endangered or vulnerable

VULNERABLE: may soon become endangered

Index